© T.F.H. Publications, Inc.

Distributed in the UNITED STATES by T.F.H. Publications, Inc., 1 TFH Plaza, Neptune
City, NJ 07753; on the Internet at www.tfh.com; in CANADA by Rolf C. Hagen Inc.,
3225 Sartelon St., Montreal, Quebec H4R 1E8; Pet Trade by H & L Pet Supplies Inc.,
27 Kingston Crescent, Kitchener, Ontario N2B 2T6; in ENGLAND by T.F.H. Publica-
tions, PO Box 74, Havant PO9 5TT; in AUSTRALIA AND THE SOUTH PACIFIC by
T.F.H. (Australia), Pty. Ltd., Box 149, Brookvale 2100 N.S.W., Australia; in NEW
ZEALAND by Brooklands Aquarium Ltd., 5 McGiven Drive, New Plymouth, RD1 New
Zealand; in SOUTH AFRICA by Rolf C. Hagen S.A. (PTY.) LTD., P.O. Box 201199,
Durban North 4016, South Africa; in JAPAN by T.F.H. Publications. Published by
T.F.H. Publications, Inc.

MANUFACTURED IN THE
UNITED STATES OF AMERICA
BY T.F.H. PUBLICATIONS, INC.

GENERAL INTRODUCTION

Undoubtedly, the vivid body color and the brilliant contrasting finnage of the many varieties of swordtails available today, coupled with their easy breeding, have been the keys for the continuing expansion of tropical fish keeping. This expansion is aquarists. Gone are the days when aquarists had to improvise essential equipment. With the development of equipment and its easy accessibility, there has also been a steady and increasing demand for information that is easily understood and not too

PHOTO BY AQUA PRESS MP & C PIEDNOIR.

Swordtails are among the world's most popular aquarium fishes. Starting with a plain green wild Mexican fish, modern man-made swordtails now are available in striking colors and with elongated fins. The anal fin of this red lyretail Simpson Hi-fin swordtail is so grossly elongated that it is no longer functional as an intromittent (fertilizing) organ.

responsible for easy access to detailed and authentic knowledge about maintaining these fishes in captivity. It also follows that there is a greater incentive toward the desire to breed these fish.

Today, fishkeeping equipment and accessories are far more plentiful and priced at a level within the reach of the majority of difficult to apply in a practical manner.

With the availability of this practical knowledge there have been alleviated many of the problems that have caused so much confusion, frustration and disappointment. To the beginner, however, there is always an air of mystery in relation to understanding why certain incidents occur. This also applies to even the more ardent and experienced aquarists. Most of these incidents are involved with efforts to breed a specific type of fish.

This book has been prepared as an endeavor to give information that will guide aquarists to attain the maximum return for their hours of devotion to this hobby of breeding swordtails.

VISUAL SEX DIFFERENCES

Sexing visually is a very difficult problem in regard to most of the egglaying species but such conditions do not apply to most species within the livebearing group. The anatomy differs greatly in the livebearing species, and these sexual differences are instantly recognizable even by a beginner. The males have the anal fin modified into a thickened tubular organ known as the *gonopodium*. Most swordtail males also have the lower lobe of the caudal fin extended. This extension is referred to as the sword, something which it closely resembles in shape. Thus the name - **swordtails**.

Female swordtails always have a greater depth of body. They also have a darkened area slightly forward of and above the vent. This area is called the *gravid spot*, which enlarges and darkens when the female is pregnant. Furthermore, the females have neither the sword-like caudal extension nor the *gonopodium*.

There are several schools of thought regarding whether or not the male during the act of copulation (mating) makes a

Brick red speckled swordtail pair. The male is the lower fish. The female is beginning to acquire a thickened anal fin as she undergoes masculinization and sex change, but she still produces offspring. See page 57 for more information on sex changes.

PHOTO BY HANS JOACHIM RICHTER.

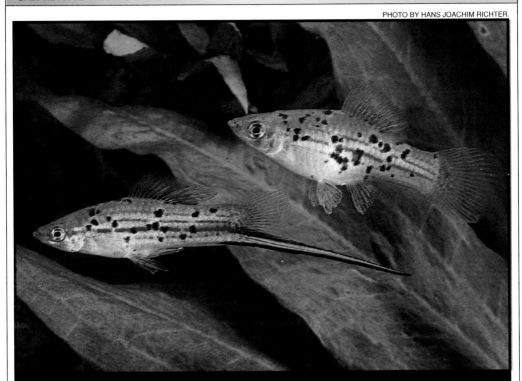

Wild *Xiphophorus helleri*. The males have extended tail fins while the female has normal anal and tail fins. The wild forms have much better body shapes and caudal extensions than do the hybrid varieties.

direct insertion of the gonopodium into the female's vent. Actually there are no known official records substantiating such an assumption, and it is assumed that actual contact is rare and unnecessary for fertilization. General belief is that the male directs his gonopodium in the general direction of her vent, and, when in close proximity, discharges the spermatozoa (fertilizing cells). The microscopic sperm enter the vent and fertilize each egg lying within the reproductive organs of the female.

Once this happens the incubation period commences. This is referred to as the period of gestation. At no time during this period does the female provide any nourishment to the developing embryos within each egg. The egg yolk contains all the food that is necessary.

The length of the period of gestation varies according to the conditions involved. These include the age of the female, the temperature of the water and general aquarium conditions. Usually this period can be estimated to be between 25 and 45 days.

The actual date of delivery cannot be definitely established, but the swollen abdomen is an indication.

In dark or black pigmented fishes, the darkening and expansion of the gravid spot is difficult to observe. In such instances the gradual enlargement of the female's body around this area is the only indication of pregnancy. The fry are usually delivered head first, but in some cases they are expelled from the female in a curved or rolled-up position.

In all instances, however, the fry will be motionless for a few to prevent this. The aquarium in which the fry are being born should contain large quantities of floating plants. These could be either Hornwort *(Ceratophyllum demersum)* or Crystalwort *(Riccia fluitans)*. If these are unavailable, the use of any of the many types of manufactured breeding traps should be employed.

PHOTO BY AREND VAN DEN NIEUWENHUIZEN.

Swordtails have been produced in dozens, perhaps even as many as one hundred, different varieties. The two females shown above show the green tuxedo pattern (top fish) and the red wagtail pattern.

seconds, then gradually sink slowly to the bottom, lie there a few seconds and then swim with difficulty to the surface. Here they take in a gulp of air and from then on are capable of swimming freely.

Swordtails are cannibalistic towards their newly born fry and it is necessary to take precautions

FOODS AND FEEDING

Many of the problems experienced by the beginning aquarist are a direct result of poor quality foods and a lack of understanding in relation to the amount of food required.

Fish maintained in captivity are always under a certain amount of duress because of lack of natural foods. In an aquarium, there is often a lack of the microscopic animal and vegetable life upon which fish depend for the majority of their sustenance. To offset this situation it is necessary to augment their diet with other foods. These can include dry foods, cultured or collected live foods or frozen foods.

mixed ingredients or an individual ingredient, should be considered as their staple diet. This should be augmented daily with at least one feeding of either cultured or collected foods. Unfortunately, the latter are only available during certain seasons. However, these may be substituted for by using the many varieties of frozen foods.

PHOTO BY HANS JOACHIM RICHTER.

There are many different colors exhibited in swordtails ranging from bright red through green and various shades of yellow and orange.

Care must be exercised not to over-feed at any one time, but the old myth about once a day feeding being sufficient is wrong. It is necessary to replenish food elements frequently.

Continuously feeding one specific type of food is not the best policy. All diets should be varied. Undoubtedly dry foods, whether

One of the best foods for development of growth and color is finely scraped frozen chicken liver. This is not only economical, but requires no special equipment for maintaining it.

However, for easier understanding the following classifications should assist:-

Dry Foods. There are numerous

name brand mixed ingredient conditioning foods available, as well as individual ingredient foods such as dry daphnia, shrimp meat, beef meal, crab meal, salmon eggs and vegetable compounds.

Home Cultured Live Foods.
Microworms *(Mikronematoderna).*
White worms (Enchytaeidae-
    Fridericia alba),
Red earthworms *(Lumbricus
    terrestris)*
Brine shrimp *(Artemia salina).*

Small beginning cultures of the first three are available at some dealers. They can also advise how they may be propagated. Brine shrimp eggs are readily available and easily cultured at home.

Collected Live Foods. These are available at certain seasons of the year and are collected from local pools, streams or rivers. The following live foods are generally very plentiful: daphnia *(Daphnia pulex),* glassworms (*Chaoborus* larvae), tubifex worms *(Tubifex rivulorum),* bloodworms (*Chironomus* larvae), mosquito larvae *(Anopheles punctipennis)* and fairy shrimp *(Eubranchipus vernalis).*

Extreme caution must be observed when collecting any of these live foods because unwanted enemies of an aquarium are certain to be present in the same water. These include water tigers (*Dytiscus* beetle larvae), dragonfly and damselfly larvae, together with parasites and fungus spores.

Never feed any live foods without closely examining them for these unwanted enemies. Any living organisms that do not resemble the actual live food collected should be removed before the live food is placed into the aquarium.

Frozen Foods. Most dealers today have stocks available of these very excellent foods, which include baby and adult brine shrimp, daphnia, bloodworms, mosquito larvae, and tubifex worms. Also available are several mixed formulas. Never feed frozen foods until you have permitted them to thaw out, otherwise many fish will immediately spit out his food, mainly because it is cold. Frozen foods decompose very quickly, and, therefore, the process of thawing-out should be done immediately prior to feeding. Never thaw frozen foods and leave them for several hours before feeding-this may cause you many problems.

Another frozen food that is very valuable is chicken livers. These should be frozen in their raw state and finely scraped before feeding. Most livebearers prefer a small amount of vegetable matter in their daily diet. The best method to provide this is through finely scraped frozen raw spinach.

It is very important that a properly arranged feeding schedule should be planned. Improper feeding invites problems to arise.

Uneaten foods, caused by overfeeding, quickly decompose in a water temperature of 70 Fahrenheit. This will also cause problems as the decomposing foods are ideal breeding grounds for harmful bacterial colonies. Visual signs of overfeeding are that the gravel or sand turns black, or the water has a very pungent odor, usually of a sulphurous nature.

Experts are in general agreement that a wholesome daily diet is the key to success in maintaining and breeding fish successfully.

AQUARIUM CONDITIONS

All livebearing species enjoy better health and growth when the aquarium conditions are correct. For the past decade there has been an over-emphasis towards having crystal clear water.

Most livebearers inhabit the estuaries and coastal shorelines where the water is murky, has an amber tinge and contains more salt than interior rivers and lakes.

Much municipal water is either neutral or slightly alkaline but generally very hard, far too hard for many tropical fishes.

All livebearing species require a slightly hard alkaline water and will readily adapt themselves to new surroundings if the pH is between 7.0 and 7.4. The DH should read between 6 and 8 degrees (equivalent to approximately 100 and 140 p.p.m.).

Should the water when tested with test kit show an alkaline reading, the best method to bring it to the desired acidity is to use a small amount of peat moss. This is placed in a piece of nylon and suspended in one corner of the aquarium. Daily tests will soon disclose when the desired degree of acidity has been attained. The peat moss should then be removed. This arrangement also will give an amber tinge to the water.

If the water is too hard, this hardness can be reduced by using a water softening filter like those available at most retailers, or by adding demineralized water that can be obtained from the local manufacturers specializing in producing distilled or demineralized waters for drug houses and hospitals.

Water temperature is very important. This should be maintained at a constant level between 70 and 78 F., with an optimum of 72 F.

Many livebearers can withstand a fairly large temperature range, but for healthy fish the optimum of 72 F. has been found to be most suitable.

PHOTO COURTESY OF AQUARIUM PHARMACEUTICALS.

The swordtail aquarium needs to have its water monitored to be sure it is within the tolerable limits of pH, hardness, etc. Pet shops sell kits to monitor and adjust water chemistry.

Most livebearing species are very susceptible to sudden changes in water conditions. Always make a comparison test when new fish are purchased and any differences between the water in which they arrive and that of the aquarium to which they are to be placed should be rectified before placement.

Shock from sudden water changes may cause them to react and develop "Shimmies." It can also affect their ultimate breeding potential.

the leaves will become coated with fine layers of algae. This is enjoyed by livebearers.

These small foliage plants include any of the following:- cabomba *(Cabomba caroliniana)*, hygrophila *(Hygrophila polysperma)*, myriophyllum *(Myriophyllum hippuroides)*, ambulia *(Limnophila sessliflora)*, vallisneria *(Vallisneria spiralis)*, sagittaria *(Sagittaria subulata)*, and ludwigia *(Ludwigia natans)*. Many expert breeders have a theory that livebearers do much

PHOTO BY EDWARD TAYLOR.

Swordtails are best kept in heavily planted aquaria so the babies can hide and females can find refuge from overly aggressive males. The fish shown here is a new variety called a *Neon Lyretail Swordtail.*

PLANTS AND PLANTING

Plants and planting arrangements differ slightly from those required for egglayers. Most livebearers are at least partially vegetable eaters, and greens should be included in their diet. By using the small foliage plants there is a greater potential that

better in aquaria that are planted only with water sprite *(Ceratopteris thalictroides)*.

In breeding aquaria, there must be a plentiful supply of floating plants such as hornwort *(Ceratophyllum demersum)* or crystalwort *(Riccia fluitans)*. The fully submerged plants should be arranged in dense thickets at the back corners. This affords an opportunity for the females to use them as hiding places against the aggressive attention given by the males.

The floating plants provide an ideal hiding place for the fry and

DISEASES AND REMEDIES

Failure to understand the basic requirements for aquarium management is responsible for most diseases. Poor conditions are responsible for bacteria and other organisms causing a variety of diseases.

Decorative items to be used in the swordtail aquarium should be designed specifically for aquarium use. Non-aquarium designated decorations could poison the water. Pet shops carry a complete range of beautiful aquarium decorations.

prevent their parents from indulging their cannibalistic tendencies and eating the young as they are born. Experiments have indicated that the use of large quantities of floating plants in the breeding aquarium is preferable to the use of the manufactured plastic breeding traps. Many females appear to withhold their young when placed in a breeding trap and undoubtedly this is because it is artificial, whereas large quantities of floating plants are more natural and similar to their native habitat.

Many diseases are of parasitic origin, the most prevalent being "white spot" caused by *Ichthyophthirius,* a disease that every aquarist is confronted with sooner or later.

Aquarium management is not essentially a matter of having crystal clear water. There are many other factors involved, such as water temperature control, ample lighting (whether artificial or natural), and proper feeding practices.

Another factor is that very few aquarists recognize the

importance of plants and far too often have too few in the aquarium. The use of healthy plants in conjunction with clean aquarium water and sufficient lighting permits the important function of photosynthesis. This is a process whereby carbon dioxide, given off by the fishes at all times, is transformed into carbohydrates, thereby benefiting fish and plants.

Too much artificial lighting or direct daylight causes uncontrolled and unsightly algal growths to appear on the plants and sides of the aquarium. Furthermore, the heat from the bulbs causes the water temperature to increase during the period of their use.

Fluctuating water temperatures are very undesirable, causing the internal glandular processes of the fishes to operate out of balance. This condition will also be caused by drastic changes in the pH and DH of the water.

Fish experiencing the discomforts caused by these various changes automatically become weakened, a condition from which they can easily become prey to both external or internal diseases.

PHOTO COURTESY OF AQUARIUM PRODUCTS.

The once tedious task of making necessary, frequent water changes which are essential for the health of swordtails, has been made easy by the automatic water changer. These handy accessories are available at your local pet shop.

In most diseases of fishes there is a period of development which cannot be visually seen and therefore impossible to diagnose.

When fish show signs of distress, it may be presumed that they are infected with some disease. External diseases usually are easily visible and can be correctly diagnosed immediately.

In the treatment of most prevalent diseases of fishes, there are available time-tested medicants that can be purchased at very little cost and without the necessity of acquiring a doctor's prescription before being able to get them at the local drug store.

For many years it has been advocated that heavy concentrations of common salt solutions are a cure-all. There are instances where such a solution may be useful, but generally speaking this should be considered one of the bogies of the early era of the hobby. Livebearers are not affected by moderate salt solutions, but there are many species of egglayers that cannot tolerate the slightest amount of salt in their water.

The following suggestions have been thoroughly tested through the medium of controlled experiments and found capable of producing an effective result without injury or harm to either fish or plants.

White spot *(Ichthyophthirius).* This disease is of parasitic origin, requiring several days before it can be diagnosed visually. It is caused by the parasitic protozoan *Ichthyophthirius multifiliis,* present in most aquarium waters. This parasite cannot attack a healthy fish, and in most instances it attacks weakened fish that have been subjected to a sudden and drastic drop in the water temperature. There are also occasions where fish may be weakened by an unclean condition within the aquarium.

The sudden drop in water temperature or an unclean aquarium condition causes the fish to suffer shock. This shock prevents the functioning of the glands that control the production of the protective mucous covering of the fish's body. In this state it can be assumed it is "naked" and prone to attack by these burrowing parasites. They attack the body of the fish, burrow beneath the skin and cause an ulcerous wound.

It requires five days for the parasite to form a cyst, after which it leaves the fish's body and slowly sinks to the bottom of the aquarium. The incubation period in this state is five days and then the cysts break open, releasing another horde of free-swimming parasites.

Although there are many commercially prepared medicants that can be used to effect a cure, experience has shown that the use of quinine hydrochloride is very effective and without any after-effect to both fish and plants. The dosage is five grains to each ten gallons of water and this dosage may be repeated again in three days if no appreciable decline in the disease is apparent. Once the white spots have disappeared from the fish, it may be presumed that a cure has been effected. However, it is essential that the remaining parasites in the aquarium water should also be liquidated.

Fin and Tail Rot. This is probably the second most prevalent disease and is bacterial or fungal in origin. It is very contagious and will quickly infect other fishes in the same aquarium. The first visual indication is that the outer edges of the lobes of the caudal fin appear to become ragged and lose their

PHOTO COURTESY OF AQUARIUM PRODUCTS.

FOR BOTH FRESH & SALTWATER FISH
LIFE BEARER
ELIMINATES GILL FLUKES, FISH LICE, ANCHOR WORMS AND LEECHES

■ Scientifically Formulated
■ Effective in 48 hours or less.
■ Non Toxic
■ Will not shock fish
■ Will not discolor water.

AQUARIUM PRODUCTS

AQUARIUM PRODUCTS   GLEN BURNIE, MD. 21061

There are many remedies and preventatives available at your local pet shop to aid in maintaining the health of your swordtails and other fishes.

color. The white color increases as the disease spreads, and the infected parts of the fin rot away. There are several commercially-prepared medicants, most of which do an effective job of ridding the fish of this disease. Continue this treatment daily until all traces of the disease have vanished.

In some instances this disease will spread to an area of the caudal peduncle. In such cases do not attempt to cut this away, but swab this area well with the solutions as already prescribed.

Mouth Fungus *(Chondrococcus).* This disease is more serious and contagious than Tail Rot. It will quickly infect all fishes in the aquarium. However, it can be treated and cured, but great care must be undertaken when treatment is given. This disease reacts similarly to medications, as does fin and tail rot. Just follow the directions listed with the medication to get the most effective results.

Cotton Wool Fungus *(Saprolegnia).* This disease is often the aftermath of other diseases which have left the fish in a weakened condition. In this state the mold spores can easily attach themselves to the sides of the fish. In this instance, this disease will not attack healthy fish and therefore infected fishes do not have to be isolated.

Use a commercial anti-fungal medication for best results and make sure to do a water change (20%). Remove any carbon from your filter before beginning treatment. Repeat daily until the fungus has entirely disappeared.

Velvet *(Oodinium).* This disease seldom attacks livebearers, but is more prone to attack Asiatic species of egglayers. There are several prescribed remedies, many of which are highly effective at treating this disease.

Nervous or Chemical Prostration. Nervous prostration occurs when fish are abused and subjected to shock. This can be in the form of the sudden immersion of a net or hand into the aquarium, drastic changes in water conditions, or being chased by larger fish continuously.

The only possible remedy is to remove the fish and isolate it for a few days in an aquarium with very subdued lighting. There the diet should consist mostly of live foods. Fish suffering from this condition usually are not very active, preferring to mope around the bottom of the aquarium. The fins are folded and sometimes there is a slight sideways movement of the body when the fish is stationary.

Chemical prostration is caused by sheer neglect and exceedingly poor aquarium management. When water evaporates, the chemicals remain in the aquarium; therefore, the continuous replenishing with fresh water to replace that which has evaporated only causes additional chemical concentration in the aquarium water. Over a period of several months this build-up becomes a dangerous problem that has toxic properties for both fish and plants. The symptoms for this condition are easily detected visually. The fish are not interested in any foods offered and remain at the lower levels of the aquarium. They seldom swim about and all fins are folded. When this happens, immediately remove 30-40% of the water and replace with fresh

evaporated water with either distilled or demineralized water. Some aquarists have the ill-conceived idea that leaving water to stand on a counter top to "age" is proper. This process does not remove any of the dissolved

PHOTO COURTESY OF JUNGLE LABORATORIES.

All of the most common aquarium fish diseases and ailments, including parasite control, can be treated with easy-to-use remedies available at your local pet shop.

tap water. This new water should have a temperature the same as that remaining in the aquarium.

Within a few hours, the fish will revive and start swimming around and accept food ravenously.

To guard against this happening, always replenish the

mineral salts; the only function of permitting water to stand is to permit the chlorine content to evaporate from it in gaseous form.

Remember, most diseases emanate from two sources, poor aquarium management and introduction into the aquarium of diseased new fish, plants or live foods.

While many black swordtail varieties stay healthy, most develop a cancer called *melanoma*. The authors studied the inheritance of melanomas in fishes and proved that this cancer was hereditary. This was a startling discovery in the late 1940's! Fish produced by Ed Parker Tropicals.

PHOTO BY EDWARD TAYLOR.

VARIETIES OF SWORDTAILS

PHOTO BY EDWARD TAYLOR.

Brick red swordtail pair. The male is on top. His tail extension is very short when compared to the wild fish...but then again, no red swordtails exist in nature! As the male grows older, his tail extension will get longer. Fish by Imperial Tropical Fish Farm.

A pair of wild green swordtails. The male's tail extension will become even longer as the fish gets older.

A blood-red male swordtail. These fish are also called *velvet reds* by the aquarium trade. Fish produced by the Moonlight Fishery.

The exceedingly popular swordtails are very beautiful fish but, strange as it may seem, the natural swordtail is far from being as glamorous as some of the many colored varieties that have been developed.

The wild *Xiphophorus helleri* could be considered as having a drab color. The general body is silvery-gray with a yellow shadow patch extending horizontally on each side. Within this area are two broken red lines. The sword-like appendage of the males is a deep yellow with a thin black edging. There is also generally a pale green overcast.

The many varieties that have been developed have been derived from careful genetic breeding for development of single color patterns. The majority of the other varieties have been accomplished through the medium of cross-breeding with *Xiphophorus maculatus*, and are actually hybrids.

There is still an enormous opportunity for improvement, and for the ardent aquarist there is a challenge.

SWORDTAIL COLOR VARIETIES

Velvet Red. These are a deep blood red, but there are two variations. One is all red, including fins and the eyes; the other has the deep red body, yellow fins and yellow sword, sometimes edged with black.

Brick Red Swords. These are a much lighter red and have the appearance of an overall yellowish sheen. Fins are yellow and the sword is yellow, sometimes without the black edging.

Red Wagtail Swords. Both the velvet red and brick red color varieties are within this group but both varieties have deep black finnage, except for the sword, which is yellow with a black edging.

Gold Wagtail Sword. The body is a deep golden yellow; fins are black, except for the sword, which is a deep yellow with a black edging. On the sides of the males there are two or three horizontal lines running the length of the body. The females have a similar marking but it is not so prominent.

Tuxedo Swords. These usually possess a deep red body along the back but are much lighter on the underside. Along the back and over the sides is a patch of deep black. This varies in size and density, but the most prized are those where the black has the appearance of a saddle.

Albino Swords. These are whitish with a yellow sheen. The irregular stripes along the side are also very indistinct. The eyes are pink and the sword is faintly edged with black. This latter color is often not shown in some specimens of this variety.

The Simpson Hifin Swords. The first seen were a medium red with the dorsal fin greatly extended in height to the point that it draped gracefully over the back of the fish as it swam. The

PHOTO BY EDWARD TAYLOR.

A pair of gold wagtail swordtails. All the fins (except the anal fin of the male) are black as are the fish's lips. Fish produced by Blackwater Fishery.

PHOTO BY EDWARD TAYLOR.

Red wagtail lyretail swordtail. This is a female changing into a male.

A pair of red albino Simpson hi-fins of poor quality. The fins are too short, but albinos are rarely well developed fishes. Albinism is the absence of black pigment.

PHOTO BY AREND VAN DEN NIEUWENHUIZEN.

A marigold crescent male swordtail produced by Blackwater Fishery.

A pair of pineapple swordtails produced by Blackwater Fishery.

PHOTO BY EDWARD TAYLOR.

.This albino is called a *red-eyed Inca gold swordtail* by its producer A&W Tropicals.

A gold tuxedo male in wonderful condition. Fish by Ed Parker Tropical Fish.

PHOTO BY EDWARD TAYLOR.

PHOTO BY EDWARD TAYLOR.

Marigold swordtail female changing to a male. Fish produced by Blackwater Fishery.

A *peppermint crescent swordtail*, female. Fish produced by Oak Ridge Fish Hatchery.

PHOTO BY EDWARD TAYLOR.

A black wagtail swordtail female. Fish produced by Ed Parker Tropicals.

Marbled swordtail, male. Fish produced by Oak Ridge Fish Hatchery.

same characteristic was developed later in red wagtail and red tuxedo swordtails as well.

From all indications it is possible to breed these beauties, but evidently they are not the prolific breeders that other varieties are.

THE SWORDTAILS

Since their introduction as aquarium fishes in 1909, swordtails have been great favorites. The known species range the Atlantic coastal waters from Mexico to Honduras. Though some of the species listed below are easy to obtain, nearly every swordtail available in a petshop is a product of a cross with the platy. Pure strains from original wild stock just do not exist in the commercial world.

A red-lace swordtail male. Fish produced by Oak Ridge Fish Hatchery.

PHOTO BY EDWARD TAYLOR.

Xiphophorus montezumae-The Montezuma Swordtail

Xiphophorus montezumae Jordan & Snyder is found in spring pools and slowly moving streams in the foothills of the Rio Tamesi, Tamaulipas, and northern tributaries of the Rio Panuco, San Luis Potosi in Mexico. It is a large swordtail with an extremely large sword. Its sword is as long as that to be found in *X. helleri* and *X. clemenciae.*

Another strain of Florida *montezumae* swordtails looks like this one.

Fish farmers in Florida call this fish *Xiphophorus montezumae*. See the section entitled *The Montezuma Swordtail Mystery* further on in this book.

A so-called *montezumae* swordtail male produced in Florida.

A Florida-produced so-called *montezumae* swordtail.

Xiphophorus cortezi-The Cortez Swordtail

Xiphophorus cortezi was described by Donn Eric Rosen as *Xiphophorus montezumae cortezi* and is found in the tributaries of the Rio Montezuma, San Luis Potosi, Mexico. Its habitat is the small streams and pools in the foothills of the Rio Panuco system. It has a much smaller sword and is a much slower growing fish than *X. montezumae*.

Xiphophorus pygmaeus-The Pygmy Swordtail

This species has two sub-species. *Xiphophorus pygmaeus* was first described by Hubbs and Gordon from the Rio Axtla, San Luis Potosi, Mexico where it hides in thick growths of aquatic weeds under the banks of fast-moving

PHOTO BY G.J.M.TIMMERMAN.

A pair of Mexican *Xiphophorus cortezi*. This is the real fish which were collected in Mexico by the authors.

Fish breeders in Japan call this the Montezuma swordtail. Notice the length of the male's caudal extension!

PHOTO BY KENJIRO TANAKA.

PHOTO BY LOTHAR WISCHNATH.

Xiphophorus pygmaeus pair, The male is the upper fish.

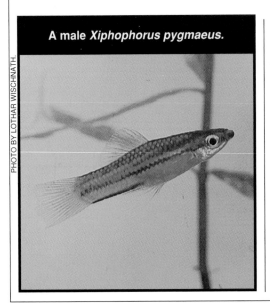

A male *Xiphophorus pygmaeus*.

PHOTO BY LOTHAR WISCHNATH.

streams. Donn Eric Rosen described a new subspecies, *Xiphophorus pygmaeus nigrensis*, (which is now considered a valid species, *X. nigrensis)* from the Rio Panuco, San Luis Potosi, but this species hides under large rocks in pools. This is one of the most difficult of the swordtails to breed and if you get a dozen babies per month you are doing fine! While *X. pygmaeus* has practically no sword at all, *X. nigrensis* has a moderately long swordtail. The tail of *nigrensis* is longer than that of *cortezi*, for example.

A pair of *Xiphophorus nigrensis* with the male showing the extension of the tail fin.

PHOTO BY LOTHAR WISCHNATH.

PHOTO BY DR. HERBERT R. AXELROD.

A pair of *Xiphophorus nigrensis* where the male shows little growth on this tail extension.

A Mexican green swordtail male, *Xiphophorus helleri*, showing the long extension of the tail fin so common only in wild fish.

PHOTO BY HANS JOACHIM RICHTER.

PHOTO BY EDWARD TAYLOR.

The Florida fish farmers are producing this strain which they call *Xiphophorus pygmaeus nigrensis*. Its true identification and origin are unknown.

A Florida produced fish the farmers call *Xiphophorus nigrensis*. This is a young female.

PHOTO BY EDWARD TAYLOR.

PHOTO BY LOTHAR WISCHNATH.

A *Xiphophorus helleri* from the Rio Nautla, Mexico. This spotted variety looks strange as the male has a short tail extension and an elongated gonopodium (anal fin).

PHOTOGRAPHED BY LOTHAR WISCHNATH.

A pair of *Xiphophorus helleri* green swordtail collected in Rio Del Reyon, Mexico.

A pair of wild green swordtails, *Xiphophorus helleri.*

PHOTO BY G.J.M.TIMMERMAN.

Xiphophorus helleri-The Green Swordtail

Of course, calling this fish a "green" swordtail is only a half-truth. Though the first *helleri* brought in were green, they exist today in many, many colors, but not in pure strains. This is the swordtail that is seen in the hobby and is the basis for this book. *Xiphophorus helleri* was first described by Heckel in 1848. It has a wide range from the Rio Nautla to the Rio Jamapa in Veracruz, Mexico. It has wide tolerances for water temperatures and habitats from near sea level to 5,000 feet up in the mountains. It can be found in almost every kind of water, from rock pools to moving streams to swamps.

Donn Eric Rosen described *Xiphophorus helleri alvarezi* from the Rio Usumacinta system in Chiapas, Mexico. This has been raised to a full species, *X. alvarezi*.

All *helleri* have beautiful, long swords and are usually very prolific.

A Florida produced green swordtail showing many of the signs of the wild ones. Fish produced by Ed Parker Tropicals and photographed by Edward Taylor.

Xiphophorus clemenciae-The Yellow Swordtail

This fish is almost unknown to hobbyists, having been available in very limited numbers only recently. It is extremely rare in nature as well and was described by Alvarez from a single range in the Rio Sarabia, Oaxaca, Mexico where it was found in a headwater stream with slight to torrential current. This species has a long sword and should be very popular once it has been developed with a high dorsal and lyretail.

In the early 1840's, the government of the old Austro-Hungarian Empire sent botanist

Florida fish farmers raised this female *Xiphophorus clemenciae.*

The fish farmers in Florida produce this fish which is called *Xiphophorus clemenciae.*

Karl Heller to Mexico to collect plants for old Vienna's Botanical Gardens. In his travels through the state of Veracruz, Heller reached Mount Orizaba, Mexico's mightiest peak (18,696 feet above the sea). In the vicinity of the village of Orizaba, at an elevation of about 4,000 feet, Heller stood amid an amazing natural display of tropical plants. With just a glance above, he could see, in the far distance, the gleaming snow-white contours of the glacial mountain peak.

An abundance of moisture, both from the torrential mountain brooks and from the mist-laden clouds that hover about the icy peak, in combination with the rich volcanic soil, has made the Orizaba region a natural botanic garden. When I was passing through Orizaba I, too, saw the huge ferns and multicolored orchids along the wayside. The colorful stalls in the market places overflowed with tropical fruits and vegetables; the odors of sweet-scented flowers and pungent spices filled the air.

Heller was skillful in his collecting in Mexico. Plant experts in Europe who worked over his botanical booty were amazed at the great numbers of new horticultural species he had found, and they named many of

Florida fish farmers raise this fish and sell it under it's name *Xiphophorus alvarezi*.

PHOTO BY EDWARD TAYLOR

Xiphophorus andersi is another of the very rare swordtails. There are perhaps a dozen species and subspecies of swordtails, mainly in Mexico. Many fish scientists look for differences (splitters) between fishes while other, more conservative ichthyologists (lumpers) look for similarities.

Mexico's famous plants in his honor. The word *helleri* appears frequently in their scientific names.

Karl Heller gathered not only plants but many small terrestrial and aquatic animals characteristic of the country. In a stream near Orizana, Heller discovered one of the most

could have been more appropriate, for the scientific name means "Heller's swordbearer."

Later, just after the turn of this century, Seth E. Meek of Chicago's Natural History Museum discovered that swordtails occur in a number of widely separated rivers in Mexico.

PHOTO BY KENJIRO TANAKA.

The Japanese are breeding this fish which is called *Xiphophorus birchmanni*.

unusual fishes in Mexico. When Dr. Jacob Heckel, the famous European ichthyologist, saw the fish that Heller brought to him for identification—dead and pickled in preserving fluid though it was—he exclaimed enthusiastically that it "was so indescribably beautiful that it must appear as something extraordinary, even to the layman." In the ceremony of entering another name in the book of the world's new species of animals, Heckel said, in 1848, "This species I name in honor of Karl Heller, its discoverer: *Xiphophorus hellerii.*" Nothing

In Northern Veracruz, right at its capital city's gates, he found a race of Jalapa (*Xiphophorus jalapae*, but this name has since been relegated to the synonymy of *X. helleri*). Then, in Oaxaca, in the great Rio Papaloapan, he found a larger race of swordtails; and in the southernmost section of Veracruz he found another swordtail colony in the Rio Coatzacoalcos, whose waters empty into the Gulf of Mexico at Puerto Mexico. It was probably at Puerto Mexico in 1909 that the lowland forms were encircled by aquarium-minded collectors and shipped first to Germany.

While Dr. Axelrod was studying with Dr. Gordon, he produced this strain of red Simpson hi-fin wagtail swordtails.

Still other swordtail tribes were found in the Rio Usumacinta and streams and lakes in the Peten and Alta Vera Pas areas of Guatemala by explorers in quest of clues to the lost Mayan civilization.

Life in the Aquarium and Laboratory

When the hobby of keeping colorful fishes from tropical waters in one's home aquarium hit at the turn of this century, there were no swordtails on the tropical fish market. Many efforts were made to find these fish, attempts stimulated by Heckel's glowing description and Meek's striking photographs of swordtails. Sailors out of Hamburg and Bremerhaven were commissioned by tropical fish importers to locate and bring back these brilliant fishes alive when their ships took them to Mexican ports.

J. P. Arnold reported in the *Wochenschrift für Aquarien und Terrarienkunde* that living swordtails were first imported into Germany in 1909. The swordtails were caught near Puerto Mexico in the Rio Coatzacoalcos. They were of a different race from the mountain forms originally discovered by Karl Heller. But they, too, were handsome animals—finer, some said, for they were larger.

From the moment the colorful swordtails and platyfish arrived in aquarium fish circles, they have been constant favorites of the amateur aquarist. From German

Right: Hand-nets are sometimes used for capturing livebearers like swordtails in the Rio Playa Vicente where Lothar Wischnath collected a strain of *Xiphophorus helleri.*

Below: A magnificently colored pineapple tuxedo swordtail, so–called by its breeder Imperial Tropical Fish Farms.

PHOTO BY EDWARD TAYLOR.

aquaria, where they multiplied rapidly, they were sent around the world. American aquarists, north of the Rio Grande, got their first swordtails not from their next door neighbor, Mexico, but from German aquarists in about 1910.

After a few years under the watchful eyes of keen fish breeders, a number of colorful varieties were established. Some enterprising aquarist discovered that platies would hybridize with the swordtails, and this mixing of species led to the creation of a still greater assortment of types both in body styles and bizarre color schemes such as the velvet reds, the blacks, and the golden and red wagtails.

I venture to say that few aquarists have seen wild swordtails as they are found in their native habitats in the rivers, lakes and ponds along the Atlantic slopes from southern Mexico, Guyana, Guatemala and the Republic of Honduras, or their direct aquarium-bred descendants. I always get much pleasure from the open-eyed amazement visitors display when they see the members of various wild stocks of swordtails. The fish are the epitome of grace, possessing harmonious patterns of shimmering greens and subtle reds.

I am amused by the strong preferences visitors express when confronted with swordtails from the Rio Blanco (probably the original *helleri* of Heckel), from the Rio Papoloapan, from the Rio Coatzacoalcos (probably the race imported into Germany in 1909), from the Rio Grijalva (the red hot one from the State of Tabasco), from the Belize River of Guyana, and from the Rio Lancetilla of the Republic of Honduras.

One feature about wild swordtails is unmistakable. In their prime they have long, well-formed swords, equal to and sometimes exceeding the length of their bodies. Hybridization with the platy has brought about a shortening of this outstanding character and thereby lessening the grandeur of the aquarium-bred commercial swordtail.

Swordtails are an adaptable species. I have caught them in rippling brooks flowing through jungles of tropical ferns and water lilies, in rubbly streams, in fast-flowing waters, where they seek the relatively slower areas behind boulders, in the still waters of upland lakes and ponds, and in gently moving clear waters of deep pools of mountain streams, where they live side by side with the platyfish.

The mountain races of swordtails are streamlined, less deep in body form than those that live in the quiet waters of a lily-pond. And yet the mountain race maintains its sleek form and the lily-pool race keeps its chunky contours in our aquaria. The racial features of swordtails are not lost in a common environment because they are genetically fixed. But they are not so different that they will not cross breed. The racial hybrids are perfect blends except for one distinguishing trait.

I found a rare black-spotted variety in several races. The

PHOTO BY EDWARD TAYLOR.

A Florida product, the green swordtail female, produced by Ed Parker Tropicals.

spotted trait is inherited in accordance with Mendelian principles. It is a dominant trait and yet it is found in less than one per cent of the population. Why doesn't the spotted variety spread through a greater number of its members? We do not know yet.

Swordtails prefer a temperature of 74 F. and a mixed diet of live and freeze-dried foods. They will not eat their young if well fed and if the babies have a place to hide in thick plants like *Nitella.* I had one female swordtail that I caught in Guyana, and put in an aquarium by herself, that gave birth to eight broods of fish, each brood about a month apart.

It has always seemed remarkable to me that swordtails taken directly out of their natural environment, particularly from rapidly flowing streams, live so well in small unaerated but well planted aquaria. No wonder it is such a good aquarium fish.

The Man-Made Varieties of Swordtails

Aside from many color varieties, there have been two very distinct varieties of finnage developed in swordtails since 1960. A California housewife, Mrs. Thelma Simpson, found some swordtails with high dorsal fins among some of her stock. By careful inbreeding she was able to fix this characteristic into what we now call the Simpson Hifin swordtail. This hifin has been bred into every known variety of swordtail *(helleri)* and platy available on the petshop market.

Another interesting sport showed up in the tanks of a Florida fish farmer named Don Adams. This was a lyretail where the upper and lower rays of the tail became elongated.

The same thing happened to the anal and ventral fins, thus making most of the males incapable of breeding since they were unable to penetrate a female with their grossly enlarged gonopodium. The way they are bred presently is by back-crossing the mothers with their sons which did not develop the lyretail characteristic. They breed about 30 per cent true by this back-cross. To date this characteristic has been limited to swordtails, no one having been able to breed a lyretail platy, but it is merely a matter of time, probably, until a similar trait shows up in platies.

Dr. Joanne Norton, a geneticist turned housewife who has a mass of aquaria in her basement, has

A red lyretail swordtail, sterile female(?) which can't seem to decide which sex it prefers.

PHOTO BY EDWARD TAYLOR.

SWORDTAIL STRAINS INCLUDE: 1. Blood red lyretail male. Photo by Dr. Herbert R. Axelrod. 2. Brick red hi-fin male. Photo by Dr. Joanne Norton. 3. Blood red Berlin lyretail male, which is a black-bodied fish with red fins. Photo by Andre Roth. 4. A pair of blood red hi-fin swordtails. Photo by Dr. Herbert R. Axelrod. 5. Brick red tuxedo male hi-fin. Photo by Andre Roth. 6. Brick red lyretail female. Photo by Andre Roth. 7. A wild *Xiphophorus cortezi* male. Photo by Hans Joachim Richter. 8. A red hi-fin male. Photo by Dr. Herbert R. Axelrod.

produced a great many varieties of swordtails and platies with combinations of hifins, lyretails, wagtails, and just about every color variety known to the aquarium trade. Her articles appeared in scores of issues of *Tropical Fish Hobbyist* magazine, and the reader is advised to study her articles in detail should he wish to embark upon a career of improving swordtail strains.

Reproduction in Swordtails

Most fishes lay eggs in order to insure the future of their species. These fishes are called *oviparous* fishes because their eggs develop outside the female's body. Goldfish, barbs, gouramis, tetras, and cichlids are examples of oviparous fishes. Certain fishes, such as pipefishes and seahorses, are strange in that the female deposits the eggs in special brood pouches in the male, and the eggs develop and hatch inside this special masculine pouch. In all oviparous fishes the egg contains a fair amount of food material (yolk) and, interestingly enough, a newborn oviparous fish weighs about 30 per cent less than the newly laid egg from which it developed, thus showing that the developing embryo used about 30 per cent of the yolk for energy to convert yolk into the cells which make up the fish itself.

Another type of reproduction in fishes and other animals is *viviparity.* In this case the egg contains little or no yolk, the developing embryo being almost completely dependent upon its mother for food. As may be

expected, viviparous fishes and animals have fewer offspring than do oviparous, and the weight of the newborn is considerably greater than that of the fertilized egg.

Swordtails, mollies, platies, and *Gambusia*, based upon the weight relationship between the fertilized egg and the newborn fish, seem to lie somewhere in between viviparous and oviparous reproduction, for the weight of the fertilized egg is the same as that of the newborn fish. Perhaps at the instant of birth the newborn fish takes in a substantial amount of water, thus offsetting the weight lost during the utilization of yolk as a source of energy for the building of tissues. The main problem seems to be in physiologically explaining how the mother swordtail is able to get food into the developing egg when there seems to be no mechanism (placenta) for a transfer of food between the parent and the developing embryo.

In the poeciliid fishes (swordtails, platies, mollies, *Gambusia*, etc.) the eggs are fertilized and develop before they have moved from the ovarian tissue from which they have emanated. In certain other livebearing fishes, the eggs develop, ripen and move into the ovarian cavity where they are fertilized and develop. Then, too, swordtails have a capacity for *superfoetation,* thus enabling them to store sperm for future generations from a single mating with a male.

Many scientists refer to the type

SWORDTAIL STRAINS INCLUDE: 1. Albino male. Photo by Andre Roth. 2. Piebald male. Photo by Dr. Karl Knaack. 3. Pair of marigold swordtails. Photo by Dr. Herbert R. Axelrod. 4. A red variegated female. Photo by Dr. Karl Knaack. 5. A pair of marigolds. Photo by Andre Roth. 6. A cancerous strain of red swordtails. Photo by Dr. Herbert R. Axelrod. 7. A healthy strain of variegated gold swords. Photo by Hans Joachim Richter. 8. The red jet swordtail showing the primary stages of cancer (melanoma). Photo by Andre Roth.

of reproduction found in swordtails as *ovoviviparous*.

There have been many different theories about how swordtails actually mate. Using slow-motion movie cameras, the author (HRA) was able to definitely ascertain that unless a prolonged actual contact was made by the male's gonopodium, no transfer of sperm was made. Swordtails breed by transferring packets of sperm, called *spermatophores*, into the female. These are fairly large and can be seen as small white masses without the use of a microscope, but a low-power lens (10x) helps considerably. Each spermatophore contains about 5,000 spermatozoa.

For breeding certain fancy varieties of swordtails, such as the lyretails and hifins, where the gonopodium might be over-developed, artificial insemination is fairly simple. To get the spermatophores from the male, simply put a male to sleep (by using MS-222) or wrap him snugly in wet cotton so he can be manipulated readily. With the male on his back, gently massage his sides the way you would "milk" the eggs from a goldfish. Then by "pumping" the gonopodium by moving it forward and backward through a 180 arc, the spermatophore will flow from the genital pore at the base of the gonopodium. By sucking them into a finely drawn syringe (pipette), and depositing them into the genital pore of the female, fertilization can almost be guaranteed for several generations of babies. The spermatophores

break apart inside the female's body, making their way into the ovarian tissue to fertilize the follicular eggs. It takes about two days for the spermatozoa to fertilize the eggs of a given brood. Sometimes the brood is born at the same time and some of the young are seen to have larger yolk sacs than others, looking like newborn egglayers. These are usually healthy youngsters and they develop as normally as their brethren.

The larger swordtails, *helleri* and *montezumae*, usually have about 75 fry at a time, though in some very mature females 175 is not to be unexpected. The time between broods of fertilized females varies between 3 weeks and 4 1/2 weeks, but almost all spawns are between the 23rd and 29th day after the previous brood. There is definitely evidence that more babies are born, and more frequently, during the summer.

In almost all cases, swordtails drop their young between dawn and three hours later. Normally it takes about 1 1/2 minutes per fry dropped on the average. Some are born head first and some tail first, and I have a video showing them being born two or three at a time.

Hybridization

For many years fish geneticists have been certain that fishes with a different number of chromosomes could not produce offspring if they could be mated. Due to the fine work of Col. Jorgen Scheel of Copenhagen this theory seems to have been exploded, for Scheel regularly

SWORDTAIL STRAINS INCLUDE: Blood red female. Photo by Dr. Herbert R. Axelrod. 2. A pair of gold tuxedo swordtails. Photo by Dr. Herbert R. Axelrod. 3. Brick red wagtail male. Photo by Dr. Herbert R. Axelrod. 4. Brick red male. Photo by Dr. Herbert R. Axelrod. 5. Wild red swordtails collected in Mexico. Photo by Dr. Herbert R. Axelrod. 6. Velvet red male. Photo by Hans Joachim Richter. 7. A pair of black Berlin swords. Photo by Dr. Herbert R. Axelrod. 8. The red tuxedo swordtail/platy hybrid male. Photo by Hans Joachim Richter.

bred killifishes (*Aphyosemion, Epiplatys* and *Nothobranchius*) with different chromosome numbers. As a matter of fact, Scheel reported that when he crossed different, but very closely related species, he found that a fish with 18 chromosomes can more easily be bred with a 9 chromosome fish than to a 15 chromosome fish. Swordtails have 48 chromosomes, while mollies and guppies have 46.

In nature, swordtails are found living together in some areas with platies, yet no one has ever found a hybrid. In the aquarium it is simple to place a male platy with a female swordtail and have hybrid fry. Of course, a male swordtail with a female platy will also produce hybrids. But, should you use a large aquarium and put in equal numbers of males and females of both swordtails and platies, hybridizing between species is very uncommon.

Further, it has been repeatedly proven that all platies and swordtails can be hybridized, but crosses between platies and/or swordtails with other livebearers such as mollies, guppies and *Gambusia*, have thus far been impossible.

Dr. Zander reports other mechanisms, too, which might keep platies and swordtails from hybridizing in nature. When he artificially inseminated swordtail females with equal numbers of swordtail and platy spermatophores, more eggs were fertilized with the swordtail spermatozoa than with the platy sperm. From 17 swordtail females he was able to produce about 1,500 swordtail babies and only about 100 hybrids.

The marigold painted sword called the *balloon*. This female was produced by Blackwater Fishery.

BREEDING FOR A TRAIT: THE RED SWORDTAIL

Visitors to New York's 1922 Fish Show were amazed by a display of twenty brilliant red swordtails, the first of their kind ever to be exhibited. Aquarists pumped their owner, a Manhattan aquarist named Mr. Silver, about their origin. Silver was determined to keep the trade secret to himself. At first he refused to talk, but when aquarists persisted in questioning him, Silver apparently yielded. "All right, I'll tell you how I got red swordtails," he said, "I bred green swordtails under a red glass cover!" This silly answer discouraged his questioners. To this day nobody really knows for sure just how Silver managed to get the first red swordtails.

I had a theory about the origin of Silver's red swordtails for I have repeatedly produced some of my own from the same basic stocks of platyfish and swordtails that were available in those days. I am not claiming any part of the credit which is justly Silver's for first obtaining, and then perfecting, his beautiful red swordtails. I wish merely to suggest how Silver might have bred them.

First it should be made clear that there are no red, yellow, black-finned, ruby-throated or tuxedo-like swordtails in the wild state (the jungle streams of Mexico and Guatemala). They exist only in our aquaria and in a sense are man-made creations.

Wild swordtails are olive-green with red confined to the zig-zag lateral line and to many dots in the dorsal fin. Every fancy swordtail on the market today, with the exception of the pink-eyed albino (which is an accidental sport), can be recreated first by hybridizing the ordinary green swordtail with an appropriately colored platy, and

Wild swordtails are olive green with the red limited to the zig-zag lateral line.

secondly by backcrossing the proper hybrid back to the swordtail, and thirdly by repeating the backcross mating for several generations.

Can you get a red swordtail by crossing a green swordtail with a red platy? In part, yes. This kind of mating will start you off in the right direction. This does not clear up Silver's mystery for there were no good, clear, red platies in his day. All the red platies at that time were known as *rubras*, and *rubra* platies had many large black pigment spots on brilliant red bodies. When a *rubra* was

PHOTO BY EDWARD TAYLOR.

A marigold twin bar (or comet) swordtail female. Fish produced by Blackwater Fishery.

mated with a green swordtail, a beautiful mottled type of hybrid swordtail was produced, but it was generally more black than red. Nevertheless, it is my guess that Silver's red swordtails were started through use of the *rubra* and here are my reasons why.

From my experience in repeatedly breeding the old fashioned true-breeding *rubra* males to gold platy females I have found occasionally the brilliant red color pattern comes through

PHOTO BY EDWARD TAYLOR.

The so-called *red lace swordtail* female produced by Oak Ridge Fish Hatchery.

to the offspring without the accompanying black spots. To be specific, this happens about once in one hundred times. Something similar happened when Silver mated *rubra* males to green swordtail females. One of Silver's swordtail hybrids came out red without black spots. This red hybrid fish was then mated back to the green swordtail, which theoretically should have produced backcross offspring fifty per cent of which were red swordtail hybrids. The better red swordtail hybrids so obtained were probably inbred, brother to sister, and from this point on the strain was well on its way to stabilization. The entire process depended upon an element of chance and then upon the perception and skill of the breeder.

An improvement in the red swordtail strain was brought about with the elimination of the green or wild element that had underlain all the red swordtails previously. This was accomplished by mating the reds to the golden swordtail strain. This resulted in the establishment of the bright blood-red swordtails. Later refinements and embroideries came to the red swordtails in the form of black fins (the wagtail type) and in the form of black formal dress (the tuxedo type). These, too, were the products of hybridization.

And now the ultimate red swordtail has been bred, one that is 100 percent red, red right down to the color of its eyes. Hints of the existence of pink-eyed red

PHOTO BY EDWARD TAYLOR.

A pineapple female swordtail bred by Victor Meyer.

swordtails began coming in about 1940; a few were being bred locally around New York City.

When I saw Henry's ad in the March, 1942, *Aquarium* announcing the "NEW VELVET RED HELLERII, WITH PINK EYES THAT GLISTEN LIKE OPALS," I hiked out to Woodhaven, Long Island, to see the aquarist, Fred Flathman, who was supplying Henry's with the new swordtails.

PHOTO BY EDWARD TAYLOR.

A lovely blood red swordtail male. The fish was raised by Ekk-Will.

Unlike Silver, who never revealed his methods, Flathman told me every detail in his long painstaking work. There were many items of human interest in his story. At one crucial point, a mysterious parasitic disease nearly wiped him out; yet, curiously, Fred looks back upon that episode, now, as a lucky break for him, because that disease left him with a few extremely hardy fish. And it is to

The so-called *red-eyed gold Inca sword* is a red albino. Fish produced by A&W Tropicals.

that disease-resistant strain that Fred attributes his present vigorous stocks.

Flathman started out with black-eyed red swordtails. Genetically they may be represented by the symbols $RR\ II$. He had to retain the red factor, RR, as is, but had to substitute the recessive pink-eyed factor, ii, for the dominant black-eyed factor II. In other words, he had to develop a swordtail with a genetic formula of $RR\ ii$.

Wagtail Swordtails

Once the development and mass production of the brilliant wagtail platyfish was accomplished, fanciers began a series of matings in an effort to adorn the decorative red and black swordtails with the same color contrasting pattern. In time these radiant types, too, were costumed with the black lace-like pattern of the wagtail and now they are available in every petshop.

Anyone who knows the platy-

swordtail group of cyprinodont fishes knows that they are closely related, despite their apparent superficial differences. Aquarists knew long ago that the platy would hybridize readily with the swordtail and that many of their hybrids are fertile. Since hybridization between platies and swordtails was possible, it was easy to predict that the wagtail pattern of the platy could, and eventually would be transferred to the swordtail. This has now been accomplished. The breeding procedure was not particularly involved, but it was time-consuming because eight months separated the generations.

The diagrams show how the golden wagtail swordtails were bred. Later, the colorful bright red swordtail was added to the wagtail category; still later the striking golden-backed, black-banded swordtail was developed. Finally the tropical fish breeders released a grand combination of all the previous color patterns— one that is red, black-banded and has black lace trimmings.

A green wagtail produced by Sanchez Bros. Tropical Fish.

The most vigorous and long-lived swordtails are those which lack the black band, for the black swordtails are inclined to come down with melanotic (black) tumors. These tumors are definitely not infectious to other fishes and certainly not to man.

Drawing the Blueprint for a New Swordtail

Mystery surrounds the origin of many domesticated varieties of fishes, but there is no mystery behind the breeding steps which produced the first wagtail platies; and there is no secret about the new wagtail swordtails.

FIRST STEP

For the first step in what turned out to be a rather long series of matings, a wild comet platyfish was paired with a wild swordtail. Anyone looking at these basic types could not possibly have predicted that the wagtail pattern would come out of such a combination, for the comet platy merely has a black line along the upper and lower borders of the tail fin; all the other fins are free of black pigment. Yet the hybrid offspring of the comet platy and the swordtail have black tails, black dorsal, black anal, and black pectoral fins; even their snouts are black.

SECOND STEP

Just as soon as this unexpected pattern was attained, fish-fanciers blueprinted a black-finned swordtail on a golden body, a color scheme that is popular in the wagtail platy. To achieve his aim, the breeder mated the black-finned hybrid to a golden swordtail, a commonly available variety. Fish fanciers have learned that it makes little difference whether the pure swordtail male is mated to a female hybrid or whether the mating is made in the

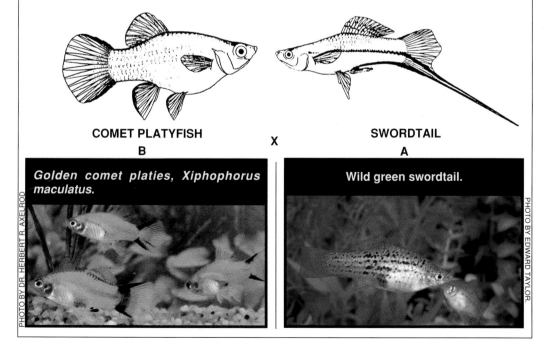

COMET PLATYFISH
B

X

SWORDTAIL
A

Golden comet platies, Xiphophorus maculatus.

Wild green swordtail.

PHOTO BY DR. HERBERT R. AXELROD

PHOTO BY EDWARD TAYLOR

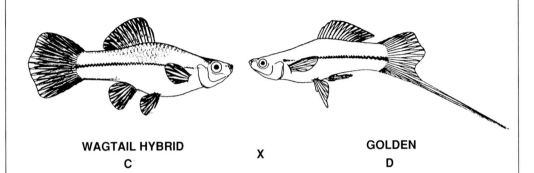

WAGTAIL HYBRID
C

X

GOLDEN
D

Wagtail hybrid. Fish bred by Imperial Tropical Fish Farm.

PHOTO BY EDWARD TAYLOR.

Golden swordtail female. It doesn't matter in crossing wagtails and golden which is the male or female.

PHOTO BY EDWARD TAYLOR.

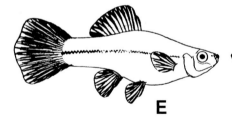

E

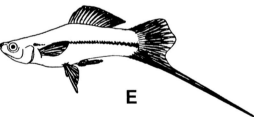

E

GOLDEN WAGTAIL
E

X

SWORDTAIL
E

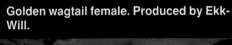

Golden wagtail female. Produced by Ekk-Will.

PHOTO BY EDWARD TAYLOR.

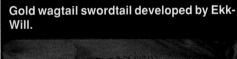

Gold wagtail swordtail developed by Ekk-Will.

PHOTO BY EDWARD TAYLOR.

opposite manner. The breeders set up many pairs and use both mating systems, hoping that some of the hybrids will produce young. The fanciers know that although platies and swordtails have the same number of chromosomes in their germ cells, sterility of some hybrids often prevents the execution of the blueprint plans. The more matings that are set up, the better the chance of attaining the desired results. The geneticist knew in advance that if he was successful in getting them to breed he would not, immediately, get golden wagtail swordtails. This was borne out by actual practice. What he expected and eventually did get was uniformly wild-colored or green swordtail-like fishes, but half of them had the wagtail pattern.

THIRD STEP

The fish geneticist also knew in advance that if he mated two of the wagtail wild-colored swordtail-like fish to each other he could count on getting three golden wagtails out of every sixteen young produced. This, too, was borne out by actual practice. If the broods are large, the problem of getting fertile golden wagtail swordtail-like fish is easy, and, merely by inbreeding, a new strain may be established by constantly selecting those golden wagtails which approach the swordtail in appearance.

THIRD STEP (AN ALTERNATE METHOD)

The fish fancier acquainted with Mendel's principles of inheritance also knew of a method which would produce a greater proportion and thus a greater yield of golden wagtail swordtails than that outlined in Step Three. It was this: a wild-colored wagtail swordtail hybrid (obtained from Step Two) was mated to a pure golden swordtail. This mating, as expected, produced one golden wagtail swordtail in every four young fish born.

Essentially, what the fish breeder has accomplished is this, and it is remarkable if one reflects upon it: he has transferred a pattern (the comet) originating in one species, the platy, to the chassis of another species, the swordtail. In the process, the pattern was changed somewhat (to the wagtail) but fundamentally the wagtail is nothing more than the glorified strain of the comet.

The Montezuma Swordtail Mystery

There are two different kinds of swordtails that have been called "montezumas" by aquarists. One is a big orange-red fish with a large dorsal fin and a long sword with three or four irregular rows of large black spots running the length of its body. Back in 1914 when this new color sport first appeared, the aquarium authority, Christian Bruning, then editor of the German magazine, *Wochenschrift für Aquarien und Terrarienkunde*, believed that it was not just a new, distinctive color phase of the common swordtail, *X. helleri*, but a representative of a different species, *Xiphophorus montezumae*. Bruning's colleagues, Arnold, the author, and Hartel, the commercial aquarist, tried to convince Bruning that he was wrong, that the red

PHOTOS BY M. BREMBACH.

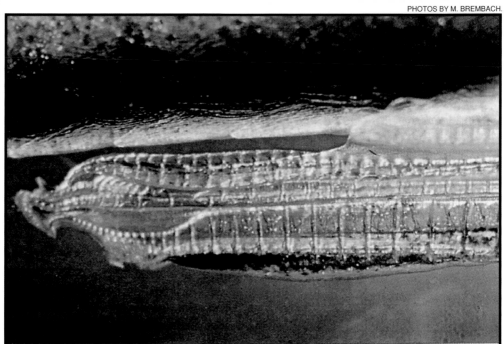

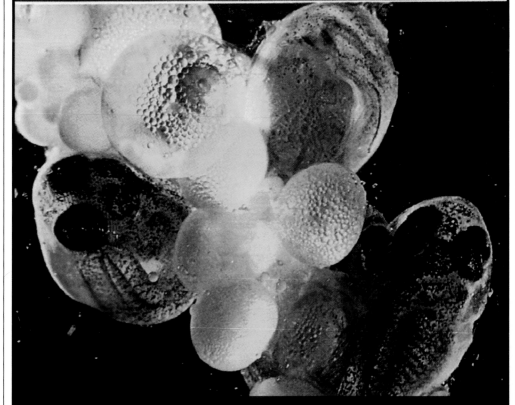

The upper photo shows a closeup of the male swordtail's anal fin (gonopodium). The lower photo shows embryos ready to hatch and eggs in various stages of development. One fertilization can produce many broods.

black-striped swordtail was a color variety of *helleri*, but Bruning was the editor-in-chief and his opinion prevailed.

This case of mistaken identity was not corrected until 1932. In March of that year the real *X. montezumae* was first brought to the attention of American aquarists by our expedition to Mexico. We shipped about twenty pairs from the Rio Axtla in the State of San Luis Potosi. The real *X. montezumae* has merit as an aquarium fish, for it is prolific and attractive in a subdued sort of way. The better males have brilliant lemon-yellow dorsal and caudal fins; their swords are smaller and have a peculiar tendency of turning up at the end. Many, but not all, of them are spotted but none of them are red.

On the Origin of the False Montezuma

Some fanciers claimed that this black-spotted, red variety originated in the aquarium as a hybrid between the common green swordtail and a red, black-spotted platyfish. They further claimed that it was perfected by backcrossing the black-spotted hybrid to the swordtail. When such a breeding program is followed, however, the false montezuma is not produced, but black-spangled hybrids with large black tumors are. Furthermore, when the black-spotted hybrid was backcrossed to the swordtail, their offspring developed still greater black tumors.

Peculiarities of the False Montezuma

The false montezuma is a peculiar fish in that it does not breed true—they always throw plain green swordtails to the extent of one-third of the brood. The false montezumas are also extremely slow in attaining sexual maturity, requiring two or three years, and some individuals apparently never grow up sexually.

Infertility and delayed maturity in a common group of animals may indicate that they are of hybrid origin. But swordtails in nature sometimes have these peculiarities too. In the Rio Bejucos near Jalapa, Veracruz, Mexico, at least half the swordtails in natural populations are gigantic infants requiring two or three years to reach sexual maturity after reaching their ordinary adult size. As there are no platies in these rivers, these huge infant swordtails cannot be hybrids. These facts, of course, do not diminish the argument that the false montezumas may be of a hybrid origin, but this criterion by itself is insufficient to establish the point unequivocally.

Breeding Performance

When the false montezumas reach sexual maturity they do not hesitate to mate with other color varieties of *X. helleri*. Results of matings with the golden swordtail are quite revealing. The large black spots so characteristic of the false montezuma seem to disappear in some of their golden offspring almost completely. But by a suitable mating the full force of the black spotting in the golden type may be restored in the members of the next generation by mating the golden false montezuma to the ordinary green swordtail. Actually these experiments indicate that two hereditary units interact and produce specific effects. For example, the gene for black spots interacting with the golden gene produces hardly any black spots. When the wild gene replaced the golden gene, the gene was able to produce many black spots on the body.

Pseudomontezuma

The German aquarist Ahl tried to resolve the confusion in montezuma terminology by naming the false montezuma *Xiphophorus pseudomontezumae*, in contrast to the name of the true one, *X. montezumae*, but this attempt to legitimize the false montezuma's name was technically illegitimate. It was not valid for several reasons: one, color varieties have no status in systematic terminology; two, there is no proof (and such proof is required) that a natural population of false montezumas exists in Mexico or in any Central American country where wild swordtails exist. The black-spotted variety of the red swordtail should be known by its popular name of "false montezuma" not by *X. pseudomontezumae*. The true *X. montezumae* (based upon the wild populations that live in Mexico) should be known under its scientific name of *X. montezumae* or under its common name as the "true montezuma."

A dealer in New York City told me that he had ordered a number of *X. montezumae* from a tropical fish breeder in Florida. Much to his

The German scientist Ahl tried to pass off this fish as a true species and named it *Xiphophorus pseudomontezumae*. But he was fooled. It was created in the aquarium!

PHOTO BY GUNTER SENFFT.

disappointment he got what he technically asked for. But what he really wanted were the false montezuma.

Solution of the Montezuma Mystery

The mysterious origin of the false montezuma swordtail has been solved in the genetics laboratory. Among the many color varieties of the common platyfish *(maculatus)* that I collected in Mexico were five, each of which had many large black pigment spots on the body or fins. One of the five is known as striped-sided because the large black pigment cells are arranged in a number of rows on the side of the body. The striped effect is not strong, and at first this color pattern was completely overlooked.

In one hybridization experiment I used a platy that had two kinds of black markings, striped-sided and spotted dorsal fin (the genetic shorthand for them being *Sr Sd)*. I crossed an *Sr Sd* platy with a swordtail and was surprised to find that 50 percent of the first generation offspring were heavily striped with black spots while the other 50 percent had strong black dorsal fins. The experiment was as follows:

P₁ (Parents)

Platy Male x Swordtail Female
Spotted-dorsal, Striped-sided
Green type
F₁ (First Generation) Offspring
50% were Spotted-dorsal hybrids:
    all females were sterile
    50% were Striped-sided hybrids:
    48% were sterile
    1% were fertile males
    1% were fertile females

There are genetic reasons why the striped-sided hybrids were females but we have not as yet been able to explain why some of the spotted-dorsal hybrids were fertile females. The reasons are rather technical and they have been published in a book, *Pigment Cell Growth*, which may be consulted if the reader is interested.

Of interest here are the striped-sided hybrids that were not only striped, but somewhat red in color. Because they reminded me strongly of the false montezuma, I thought if I could strengthen the black stripes and the red background coloring I could recreate the mysterious montezumae of Bruning. To put the plan in operation I made the following mating:

F₁ Striped-sided Hybrid x Wild Swordtail

The results were in accordance with my expectations. Still, the fish were short of perfection because the males' swords were not yet long enough, nor were they quite as red as they should have been. By taking the best of the false montezuma-like hybrids and backcrossing them to the pure swordtails, I got some that were indistinguishable from the original false montezuma.

The mystery of the origin of the false montezuma swordtail may now be said to be solved. It was created by hybridization just as Arnold suspected. The platy that was used in the original mating must have been a striped-sided fish.

THE PROLIFIC SWORDTAIL

An albino born on February 15, 1941 produced her first brood of 18 young on October 20, 1941, a second brood of 29 on November 1. This was at the abandoned New York Aquarium in Battery Park. Moved to quarters in the American Museum of Natural History in mid-November, she did not miss producing a third brood of 29 about a month later. She continued this practice of producing a brood a month apart, except for a short period of rest during the late summer, for about a year.

During this period she had two mates. The first was a "wild"-

With Green Male	Black-eyed Green	Black-eyed Golden	Pink-eyed Albino
10/20/41	9	9	
11/1/41	17	12	
11/30/41	17	12	
12/29/41	19	24	
1/30/42	20	24	
3/1/42	18	15	
4/1/42	19	18	
5/4/42	18	14	
6/5/42	19	23	
Golden Male			
9/20/42		20	17
10/22/42		16	12

These add up to 372 young all told.

If the reader has a critical turn of mind perhaps he might wonder why an albino female produced the number and kinds of young she did.

It must be clear that up to and including the brood born on 6/5/42 the sperm of the first wild colored male were effective. As a matter of record the green (wild) male was removed in March. The black-eyed golden male was introduced in August. From the facts given a geneticist can provide an explanation of the results indicated in the table as follows:

First Pairing			
Parents, P_1=Pink-eyed		Black-eyed	
Albino	x	Green	
ii stst		*II Stst*	
First Generation, F_1=	50%,	*Ii Stst,*	Black-eyed, Green
	50%,	*Ii stst,*	Black-eyed, Golden
Second Pairing			
Parents, P_1=Pink-eyed		Black-eyed	
Albino	x	Golden	
ii stst		*Ii stst*	
First Generation, F_1=	50%,	*Ii stst,*	Black-eyed, Golden
	50%,	*ii stst,*	Pink-eyed, Albino

PHOTO BY EDWARD TAYLOR

The white albino female. Albinos are available from this light to blood red. Fish produced by A&W Tropicals.

colored green male. For a period she was without a mate and later in August a black-eyed golden swordtail male was introduced.

The list of her young and their frequencies is reflected in the changing marital conditions.

Swordtail Sex Changes

Aquarists have repeatedly reported instances of "sex reversals" in some of their fishes. A survey of the reports reveals that the alleged "sex reversals" represent a great variety of changes in the appearance or in the behavior of a fish of one sex in the direction of its feminine or masculine counterpart. Under the heading of "sex reversal" many aquarists have reported that senile, female swordtails developed male-like extensions to their tail fins. Other aquarists have related how some of their female fighting fish temporarily became as brilliant as males in "war-paint," everted their gill membranes and in a reversal of behavior threatened and charged males twice their size. These changes, either of a physical or of a behavioral characteristic, are often brought about by the slight hormonal upsets that accompany advanced age. They are readily noticed, quite startling to the observer, but of little functional importance. Forthright evidence for *spontaneous, functional sex reversal* in any fish does not exist if by spontaneous, functional sex reversal the following is meant: the change in the reproductive capacity of a mother (not just of a female) to that of a father (not just of a male). This basic type of sex change is quite different from the superficial changes usually ascribed to examples of "sex reversal." Spontaneous, functional sex reversal in a fish has never been proven completely.

In order that a sex-reversed mother may eventually be able to produce effective spermatozoa like those of a potent and functioning male, her primary glands of sexuality must first be altered radically. Her once-functioning ovaries have to be destroyed or

reduced to complete impotency. Then from the residual gonad and accessory organs, testicular tissue has to be regenerated. Even this is not enough. For unless the

PHOTO BY DR. HERBERT R. AXELROD

A blood red female swordtail showing signs of sex change with the thickening of the anal fin and the slight extension of the tail.

regenerated testes are capable of producing viable spermatozoa and unless the animal develops the proper sex drive to mate, and unless the secondary sexual structures make it possible to transmit the spermatozoa to permit insemination of the eggs of another female, it is most unlikely that complete and functional sex reversal can be accomplished.

In some female vertebrate animals the ovaries are sometimes destroyed by disease; in other females, ovaries are sometimes removed by surgery. If one or the other happens to a mammal, the female becomes sterile. If one or the other happens to a hen, the bird becomes masculinized. This is because hens have rudimentary non-functional testes and male accessory organs. In ovariectomized chickens the rudimentary non-functional testes begin to develop. When the ovaries no longer exist in a hen the former supply of the feminizing hormones is radically reduced. This deficiency in a hen apparently permits the testicular or incipient male rudimentary elements to start their growth. When this happens the once-rudimentary testes produce more and more male hormones that eventually masculinizes the comb and voice of the animal. This is the biological explanation for the once mysterious phenomenon of crowing hens.

In recent times two egg-laying hens were maintained until they passed their prime as functioning females and mothers. Then, according to the report, the hens became masculinized so completely that they appeared to be similar to cocks. The transformed hens eventually attained sufficient masculinity to court and to mate with normal hens. The report said that the two erstwhile egg-laying hens later successfully fathered broods of chicks.

If this could happen to chickens, why not to fishes? Well, in 1926, Dr. J. M. Essenberg of the University of Oklahoma reported that two female swordtails which he claimed previously had many young transformed into functional males and fathered the young of other females.

Before evaluating the evidence for Essenberg's claims of the spontaneous and functional sex reversal in two female swordtails some background information concerning sexual behavior and reproductive physiology of both sexes is helpful.

In order to mate, the male swordtail must have not only functional testes, but the testes must be able to produce perfect *spermatophores*, that is, spermatozoa in "pellet" form. In order to deliver the pellet-like spermatophores to the genital pore of the female at the time of mating the male must have a functional gonopodium because insemination is internal in this as in other viviparous species. But even though the gonopodium may be perfect, this organ cannot function properly and precisely without its elaborate internal skeletal supports known collectively as the *gonopodial suspensorium*. In addition, the gonopodium and its suspensorium must be activated by elaborate sets of specialized muscles.

In the normal growth of a female swordtail many of the essential anal fin skeletal supports that might have formed the gonopodial suspensorium are dissolved at the time of the female's maturity and then the bones are completely eliminated. This serves, in part, to make room within the body cavity for the many developing embryos (sometimes 200 of them) in the ovary. Without these internal bony supports (to which in normal males special and powerful muscles are attached) it is unlikely that the gonopodium of the masculinized female could move with the extreme precision required of it at the time of mating.

Further, in testing any masculine-like female swordtail for its possible male reproductive ability, virgin females are essential. This requirement is easier to state and recommend than to accomplish because of the female's ability to store spermatozoa within the folds of her oviduct for as long as eight months. Once the female has been exposed to a normal adult male swordtail, she should never be used to test the potency of a second male or male-like female swordtail. Therefore the history of all females used must be completely known and must meet the rigid requirements demanded in tests of this sort. One sure practice of obtaining virgin female swordtails is the removal, almost daily, of potential males from a common aquarium. Males, when immature, are characterized by the thickening and lengthening of their anal fins and by the elongation of the lower part of their caudal fins. Another method used to obtain virgin swordtails, of course, is the isolation of young fish one to a container almost from the time of their birth.

With these generalities as a background, let us examine the two alleged cases of spontaneous functional sex reversal in two swordtails as reported by Dr. J. M. Essenberg in the 1926 Biological Bulletin. Their re-evaluation is particularly necessary because these two cases have been accepted widely and without qualifications in nearly every text-book in zoology that discusses the subject of sex reversal.

Early in the spring of 1923 Essenberg, then working at the University of Missouri Medical School in St. Louis, received some swordtails from two sources: from a stock maintained at the University of Chicago, and from those raised at the Crescent Fish Farms of New Orleans. For some unexplained reason, the fish from these two sources were first mixed and then each fish was isolated. The number of females Essenberg isolated was not indicated.

On May 4, 1923, a female swordtail identified by the number "B16" gave birth to 53 young and 40 more young about a month later, June 2; after that time she did not produce any more visible young. On September 12, 1923, according to Essenberg, swordtail B16 "reached advanced stages of sex reversal" but just what these changes were was not described. After this date a break in the continuous identity of swordtail B16 is definitely possible. Essenberg said that swordtail B16 (together with other fish) was shipped from the University of Missouri Medical School to the University of Oklahoma School of Medicine at Tulsa. On December 1, 1923, a swordtail male which he identified as the same B16, was mated to a virgin female swordtail. (At this point one could question the virginity of the fish used, since it is not explained what methods were used to obtain them.) On February 25, 1924, according to Essenberg, the fish identified as B16 and its mate produced 8 normal young; three of the eight were reared to sexual maturity; one was a male and two were females.

This is all the information that was published concerning the swordtail B16. Nothing was said about its reproductive behavior in the presence of a normal female. Nothing was described of the condition of its gonopodium, nor of the condition of its reproductive glands. Therein lies good cause for doubt of the actuality of the event.

Essenberg's second alleged spontaneous, functional, sex-reversed fish appeared in a second lot of swordtails among "adult females not less than 3 years of age" shipped to him by the Crescent Fish Farms at an unspecified date. It is not clear how their ages or sex were determined accurately.

Four old "female" swordtails from the Crescent Fish Farms were regarded by Essenberg as noteworthy. One "female," C32, which had not produced any living young subsequent to its arrival at his laboratory "transformed into a male" according to Essenberg, but he described no evidence of an external nor internal nature in the C32 swordtail in support of his statement.

Another female, C14, which allegedly produced "three litters" later, according to Essenberg, transformed into a "male"; it, however, was unable to function as a male when paired with a virgin female swordtail.

The third outstanding adult female swordtail, C3, cited by Essenberg, gave birth to one litter, after which C3 transformed into a "male." When mated to a "virgin" female, Essenberg said, the pair produced two male and three female young.

In none of the three unusual swordtails were post-mortem examinations made of the gonads or other internal organs. This was not because of lack of facilities, nor lack of appreciation of the kind of evidence that would be required to substantiate the claims of radical sexual deviation. For example, another swordtail, C14, of undesignated history, was autopsied and the diagnosis was made that it had spermatophores in well-formed testes but its sperm duct was obstructed.

That is all we have to go on to decide the reality of the alleged sexual changes. If I were a member of a jury passing on the evidence for spontaneous, functional sex reversal in two swordtails and for somewhat less radical changes in four others, I would have doubts, lots of doubts, as to the validity of any of them.

From the thousands of swordtails and platies that have been reared (like guinea pigs) in various laboratories for more than a quarter of a century since 1926, and from the thousands of fishes that have been reared elsewhere, no additional cases of *spontaneous sex reversal* have been reported and substantiated during the past twenty-five years. Many instances of reversal in *secondary sexual characteristics* such as changes in finnage and coloration and in behavior have, of course, been reported in the swordtail and in other fishes, but these are not more significant of fundamental sex change than may be found in a bearded lady, or in a bald one for that matter. (Curiously beardedness and baldness, apparently opposite abnormal conditions, are engendered by hormonal upsets. The same applies to fin changes in swordtails.)

Categorical claims that a swordtail or some other species of fish had functioned as a female and then transformed into a functional male have been made, but investigations of alleged spontaneous and functional sex reversal reveal that either the female had never actually been a mother, or the transformed male had never been a father. It is quite difficult but essential to provide verifiable evidence on both of these fundamental counts.

In view of the looseness of labels used in describing sexual deviants it would be better to reconsider the usage of the term "sex reversal." Perhaps the expression "masculinization" may carry all the meaning necessary to express the change in a particular character in an abnormal fish. For example, male-like anal fins or gonopodia are occasionally developed in female livebearing fishes. In two instances that have come under my observation, the gonopodium-bearing platy females continued to bear young, just like normal females. This was not a case of sex reversal, but a case of spontaneous masculinization of the anal fins. This condition may now be experimentally reproduced in female livebearing fishes by first amputating their anal fins and than applying appropriate quantities of male hormones during the period of the fin's regeneration.

When male hormones are carefully administered to immature female guppies or platies, the treated fish will eventually develop into fish that have all the appearance of males including their urge to chase, to court and to attempt to mate with normal females. But they can go just so far in their newly acquired masculine behavior. They cannot consummate mating and insemination, because they cannot produce perfect spermatophores, although their gonads may produce some testicular cells. Although these fish are masculinized *almost* completely, that *almost* makes all the difference. Actually they are not males at all and never were.

It is conceivable that by finding just the right dose of a suitable hormone for treating immature viviparous fishes and by beginning the medication at a sensitive age, some experimenter will be able to convert an otherwise potential female into one that functions as a male.

Toki-o Yamamoto of Japan has demonstrated the possibility of doing the reverse experiment with young medakas, *Oryzias*. He converted quite young (non-functional) males into functional females by treating them with estrone or with stilbestrol. He was able to identify the immature males by their associated sex-linked characters. Normal male medakas carried one X and one Y chromosome; females carry two X chromosomes. Color genes are carried by the X or Y chromosomes.

Male XY medakas, after they were converted by estrogenic hormonal treatment to female-like creatures, were mated to normal untreated males, which carry the XY chromosomes also. The feminized male and normal male produced many young, about three quarters of which were males, one quarter were females. In other words, when a mating was conducted in which both parents were XY (that is, XY times XY) about one quarter of the offspring would obtain two X chromosomes; these were females. Most of the male offspring had the XY chromosome constitution, but some males had the unusual, but theoretically expected YY chromosomal combination. When Yamamoto mated an unusual YY male to a normal female (which, of course, was XX) he expected to get all male offspring since from the mating of YY and XX individuals the only possible chromosomal combination among the young has to be XY. Sure enough, Yamamoto obtained 72 males out of 72 young.

Yamamoto regarded his successfully feminized male medakas as examples of complete and functional sex reversal and so they were if the definition of that type of sex reversal is broadened a bit. Yamamoto made it quite clear, however, that the feminizing treatment was started on the males at an early age, long before they were able to function as males. Thus they are not examples of *spontaneous and functional sex reversals.*

Perhaps we need a more precise definition to characterize those animals which function successfully first in the capacity of one sex and then at some subsequent time function successfully in the capacity of the opposite sex. That is why the term spontaneous and functional sex reversal is used here.

Credence has been granted to a few rare examples of this type of sex reversal among the fishes and birds but unqualified acceptance, it seems to me, should wait upon more complete evidence. On the other hand, surgical castrations of female Siamese fighting fish have, in several instances, produced fish in which the regenerated gonad was a functional testes. Castrated female individuals with testes became more colorful and aggressive and successfully embraced normal females during mating. They were fully able to produce viable spermatozoa which in turn effectively fertilized the ova released by the normal females. These experiments were first performed in the United States by Noble and Kumpf in 1936. Later, the results of these experiments were fully confirmed in 1951 in Germany by Kaiser and Schmidt, who worked independently of previous knowledge of similar work. Indeed, the latter did not refer to the work of the American workers.

No doubt my remarks questioning the evidence for spontaneous, functional sex reversal in viviparous fishes, particularly the swordtail, will in turn be questioned by some aquarists. Some will insist that they have had a fish whose sex was changed from that of a mother to that of a father. If these instances are brought to my attention I shall continue to ask the following questions in an attempt to get the fundamental evidence for a proper diagnosis:

1. How long did you have the alleged sex reversed fish in your possession and under your personal observation?
2. Did it come from a brood that was unusual in any other way?
3. Did the fish reach maturity at about the same time that its normal siblings did?
4. If the fish in question was first a female, did it mate with a normal male and produce fertilizable ova (if the fish was an egglayer) or did it give birth to living young (if it was a livebearer)?
5. How many young did it produce and what was the sex ratio among its progeny, that is, how many of its young were male, how many female?
6. What was the interval of time between the loss of the fish's feminine attributes and its first external marks of masculinity?
7. Which secondary sexual characters were changed during the transformation period?
8. How long did the complete sexual transformation take?
9. How many progeny were produced by the completely masculinized female (now acting and functioning as a male) after it had successfully mated with a normal female? Among the progeny how many were male, how many female, how many were sterile?
10. Was the normal female that had mated with the alleged completely masculinized female a virgin prior to this mating? How old was it at the time of mating? What precautions were taken to insure its prior virginity?
11. Finally, was a thorough post-mortem examination made of the alleged completely sex-reversed fish?
12. What were the findings of a microscopical examination of the condition of its gonads and accessory organs?

Scientific facts are constantly being subjected to verification and re-evaluation. Every fair-minded person must agree that unconditional evidence is required before the reality of spontaneous, complete and functional sex reversal in fish should be accepted.